BALLAD OF A
KARAOKE COWBOY

BY SANG KIM

KCLF-21
PRESS

Ballad of a Karaoke Cowboy

All original work © 2007 by Sang Kim

FIRST EDITION , 2007

Library and Archives Canada Cataloguing in Publication

Kim, Sang
Ballad of a Karaoke Cowboy / Sang Kim.

A play.
ISBN 0-9782020-2-3

1. Identity (Psychology)--Drama. 2. Korean Canadians--Drama.
I. Title.

PS8621.I5446B34 2007   C812'.6   C2007-905534-6

Publisher: Dae-Tong Huh
Design & Layout: Sandra Huh
Cover Design: Sandra Huh
Author Photograph: Colin Taylor

For all other rights contact **Korean Canadian Literary Forum-21 Press**:
PO BOX 45035   5845 Yonge St. Willowdale, ON, M2M 4K3 Canada
Phone: 416.222.7935

Printed and bound in Canada.

The Korean Canadian Literary Forum-21 Press
acknowledges the support of the Ontario Arts Council.

ONTARIO ARTS COUNCIL
CONSEIL DES ARTS DE L'ONTARIO

BALLAD OF A

KARAOKE COWBOY

KCLF-21
PRESS

To Kiki

...for as you dream you shall become...

My heartfelt thanks to Patricia Ghamami for resuscitating the play when the easier thing to do was to simply abandon it. Thanks to Colin Taylor, Susan Walker, Visjna Brcic, and Melinda Deines for foster-caring for it during the early developmental stages. The rest of the way was aided and abetted by Erin Pim and Sherry Kimura- thank you both for helping me excavate the soul of the play.

Thanks also to the cast of the original staged reading for your incisive questions and commentary.

My utmost gratitude to Nadine Sivak for reminding me why I write plays in the first place. In your hands, this most difficult of forms looks effortless.

Ballad Of A Karaoke Cowboy was originally published in a slightly different version, entitled "Loon Lake", by *Acta Victoriana* 1991, University of Toronto.

Ballad Of A Karaoke Cowboy was originally produced as a staged reading at SummerWorks Theatre Festival 2007 (Keira Loughran- Artistic Producer) at Factory Theatre on August 8, 2007. It was directed by Nadine Sivak. The production co-ordinator was Nina Lutz.

The cast were as follows:

YONG Dale Yim

KIKI Grace Lynn Kung

SHERIFF & JAMES Dan Darin Zanco

LOUIS Herbie Barnes

JONAH Darrell Dennis

CHARACTERS

YONG, *(aka* **HOPALONG CASSIDY***), Asian Man,* **early-30's**

KIKI, *(aka* **AZALEA***), Asian Woman,* **mid-20's**

SHERIFF, *Black Man,* **late-50's**

JAMES, *Black Man,* **mid-30's**

LOUIS, *Native Indian Man,* **early-30's**

JONAH, *Native Indian Man,* **early-20's**

SETTING

The setting shifts between a karaoke bar in downtown Toronto and an abandoned cabin in Northern Ontario. Nothing realistic. The karaoke stage should be simply suggested, a platform where songs are sung on a microphone with musical accompaniment or performed with a guitar. The cottage should be suggested with a trophy buck hanging from a wall, ceremonial Plains Indian headdresses, and a fake black bear rug.

Fade outs should be as brief as possible between scenes.

Songs used in the play are:
"Lady" © by Kenny Rogers
"I Walk The Line" © by Johnny Cash
"Kaw-Liga" © by Hank Williams
"Learning To Fall" © by Martina McBride

Karaoke bar.
KIKI *is sitting at a table for two. Dolly Parton's "Islands In The Stream" is playing lightly in the background. On one wall, a neon "APPLAUSE" sign, currently off.*

KIKI *(To the audience)* This is how it began- a story- about cowboy and his lady. Everything I say true. *(Pause)* James take me to karaoke bar-- say "something special" about place. James my ESL teacher.

JAMES *enters, carrying two beers.*

JAMES That bartender. I think I've met her somewhere.

KIKI It is good, yes? Meet old friend. So nice. *(Looking over at the bartender)* Your friend so beautiful. *(Gestures ballooning breasts, giggles)* So big- no? Too bad only get lucky with flat chest like me.

JAMES *(Places one of the beers in front of* **KIKI***)* That's $3.25, sweetie.

KIKI *(Taking money out of her purse. To* **JAMES***)* Sank you berry much.

JAMES *(Still gazing back at the bartender)* I think I took her home once.

KIKI Only once?

Pause.

JAMES Maybe I'm thinking of someone else.

KIKI Maybe remind you of another girl. *(Beat)* From Japan.

JAMES But she looks so familiar. *(Pause)* You're a doll. I love you.

KIKI *(To audience)*After fourteen months in English-Second-Language school-- three ESL teacher-- also boyfriends-- not trust English words. Example. Teacher say…

JAMES I love you.

KIKI Then he talk about other girls.

JAMES I think I took her home once.

KIKI Then feel guilty. So…

JAMES I love you

KIKI …again. Funny, this language-- no connection-- word and feeling.

JAMES I really do love you.

KIKI You already say once. Sweeter first time.

JAMES I want to say it to you and mean it every day for the rest of my life. *(About to kiss her on the lips)*

D.J.'S VOICE Ladies and gentlemen…

KIKI *(Turns her head to the audience)* Then it happen.

> **YONG** *enters onto the singing stage and stands behind a microphone.*

D.J.'S VOICE …join me in welcoming to the stage tonight…

JAMES There he is. What did I tell you?

D.J.'S VOICE …the legendary Karaoke Cowboy himself…

KIKI *(To audience)* Once-in-lifetime moment. Like two stars… *(Gestures with two hands coming together, fingers weaving)*…come together.

D.J.'S VOICE…singing- what'll you be singing this time, Hoppy?

JAMES Watch this. Freak…

YONG "Lady".

D.J.'S VOICE Kenny Rogers?

YONG I reckon that's the chap's name.

D.J.'S VOICE Here he is then, live at the Chuckwagon, where "Cow-bar meets Cow-grill"…Hopalong Cassidy with "Lady". Let's show him some love, folks.

> *The "APPLAUSE" sign blinks on and off.*
> *Lights dim.*
> *Spotlight on* **YONG**.
> *Music leads in.*
> *Disco ball goes on, projecting stars on the walls and ceiling.*
> **YONG** *loses himself completely into the song. His singing is too natural, too innate, to require any mannerisms in his voice. The song must be sung without caricature- played for real.*
> *The audience is invited to sing along by* **YONG**.

YONG *(Sings "Lady" by Kenny Rogers)*
Lady, I'm your knight and shining armour and I love you.
You have made me what I am and…I am yours.
My love…there's so many ways I want to say "I love you".
Let me hold you in my arms for…ever more.

You have gone and made me such a fool.
I'm so lost in your love.
And oh…we belong together.
Won't you believe in my song.

Lady…for so many years I thought I'd never find you.
You have come into my life and…made me whole.
Forever, let me wake to see you each and every morning.
Let me hear you whisper softly…in my ear.

BALLAD OF A KARAOKE COWBOY

In my eyes, I see no-one else but you.
There's no other love like our love.
And yes, oh yes I'll always want you near me.
I've waited for you so long.

Lady, your love's the only one I need.
And beside me is where…I want you to be.
'Cause my love, there's something I want you…to know.
You're the love of my life…You're my lady.

JAMES *sits frozen in tableaux, beer in his hand. The "APPLAUSE" sign blinks on and off.*
He raises his hat, takes a bow.
KIKI *stands and applauds ecstatically.*
YONG *looks in her direction and raises up his hat again with his thumb.*
Time stands still for both of them as they lock eyes.
Lights go up blindingly for a moment, then blackout on the whole stage.
The "APPLAUSE" sign continues to flicker on and off.

D.J.'S VOICE Let's hear it one more time for my man. The one, the only, the Karaoke Cowboy himself, Hop-a-long Cas-sidy!

The "APPLAUSE" sign goes off.
Lights up on **KIKI**.

KIKI *(To audience)* And that is when I knew. Everything I look for in my life-- I find here-- at karaoke bar. Everything I wish for come true. A man-- a cowboy-- like no other in the world. His voice-- his presence-- his charm-- sweep me away like broom. *(Pause)* My name Kiki. Here- *(Holding out a passport and a sheet of paper)* My passport and papers-- see- place I born—Saitama-- Japan. My birthday-- March 25, 1986. My family name- Abe. My photograph before come here. And also signature. I show you-- prove to you-- I am me-- not somebody else. If you not believe me-- here-- I have paper say. Me-- I don't care so much identity-- but here always people talking about. I not Christian-- no attachment to country-- to province-- to sports team-- to union-- no like same sex. I only follow my heart. Know myself-- that's my idea. *(Tapping herself in the chest)* I knock my own door-- not somebody else door. *(Referring to* **YONG***)* He-- Hoppy-- come from China-- but long time ago-- only a boy-- from Hong Kong. His uncle buy for him cowboy suit-- he go out for Halloween-- sing "Ten Little Indians"-- ask for candy-- spin gun on finger. Find his calling. Begin his journey. *(Pause)* In high school-- nobody like-- think too strange-- wear cowboy hat to class-- spurs on boot-- stand by himself in corner during school dance. Everyday he go home and read book about wild west-- watch western movies-- nobody ask "come outside and play"-- he read and watch everything-- then one day something happen-- like chicken bone-- from here, the breast-- snap-- nobody understand what happen-- not even doctors at mental hospital know. Finally, he leave home and school-- go to big city-- sing songs. Last time someone see him-- he go on greyhound bus-- disappear into big city. *(Pause)* He call me Azalea-- like flower. It was here-- at Chuckwagon-- I first see him-- "see him"-- no, not right way to say. At Chuckwagon I first "experience" him-- yes, experience-- is right word. Until that moment, my life nothing-- no meaning-- not real. That moment-- I learn one thing-- that my life here with him-- nobody else-- only him. I decide not go back Japan-- not work like robot in electronic factory-- die from too much work-- not marry husband I not love. I will not do it—no-- to me, not living this kind of life. I try already for twenty-one years now.

Parodying **YONG's** *country twang*

"Worn that coat for too long, darlin'", he say to me once.
I decide time for change-- no more give up on promise I make to myself--no, I change my life. He'll always be one that I love from moment I first see him.

Lights fade out. **JAMES** *exits.*
Sound of a horse whinnying.

Lights up on an abandon cabin.

YONG'S VOICE: (Off) Whoa, Topper! Easy, boy. Jus' passin' through.

BALLAD OF A KARAOKE COWBOY

KIKI *She picks up a sketch pad, looks out the "window", and begins sketching.*
KIKI *(To audience)* He coming now.

Sound of boots clomping up the steps.
YONG *swaggers in and leans up against the door frame.*
Sound of High Noon melody in the background.
He has a slight limp in his right leg, an affect he has long believed to be the result of a gunshot wound. From his waist, dropping down his thighs are two leather holsters securing a pair of pearl-handled Colt .45's. He is holding under one of his arms a large wooden plaque that has "LOON LAKE" inscribed onto it. He wipes the dust from his britches and lifts up his hat with his thumb.

YONG Azalea, darlin', I swear you's getting' purtier by the minute. I think this cool weather's doin' ya some good. Nice gettin' shut of all that city smoke and fillin' our lungs with some ole fashioned country air, ain't it? *(Holds up the sign for her to look at)* Never can tell what you'll find when you go ramblin' round a place like this. Says here…"LOON LAKE" …Reckon they's loonies about. Ain't seen a single one since we drifted on in here. I calculate this Loon Lake is one tough situation, though. Unneighbourly beasts of every sort in this neck o' the woods. *(He puts down the sign. Taking off his boots. Suspiciously)* See any Injuns about?

KIKI Engines. "Machines consisting of parts, working together in unison." Yes, engines.

YONG Not "engines", darlin'. Injuns. In-juns. I 'magine we're in Apache country by now. Hell, I don't aim to get us into any mess with Injuns if I can help it. There's no telling what's in the mind of an Injun. Yet sundown ain't too far off, an' no 'Pache in his right mind would fight at night. *(Stuffing dry grass into his boot)* An ole Injun' trick. Saw a 'Pache do it down by Chicorica Creek once that winter o' the blizzard. Helps keep 'em dry. *(Pause)* You sketchin' agin? Seems sketchin' is the only thing that stirs your fancy. The nurses from the bin, hell they just asked me at the ranch earlier today if you wasn't some artist, seeing as how you seem so fixed on that sketchbook o' yers. *(He walks over to her and sneaks a peek over her shoulder.)* You shor' can sketch a mean scene, though. *(Looks out the "window", then back at her sketch book.)* Damn good mock-up of the real thing if I ever seen one. I worry 'bout you, though. You're gonna go stale with jus' settlin' around and sketchin' all day. Why don't you and I mosey on out for awhile? The air's nice and crisp out there. Makes the insides of yer nose feel like a frozen spiderweb ever'time you breathe.

KIKI Breathe. "Take air into and expel it from the lungs."

YONG Heh, that's right. Yor english getting' better ever'day. I can almost understand you by now. *(Walks around the cabin chewing on a piece of hay)* I'm beginning to find this place much accomodatin'. H'bout you, Azalea? Findin' this place to your comfort?

KIKI Comfort, yes.

YONG Glad to hear it. I reckon we can set around for a wee while before lighting out agin.

The lights take on the pinkish hue of sunset.

YONG The sunset is just on the other side of the lake. Them nurses and the town Sheriff are probably looking for us by now. But don't you worry yourself to death, with me in the saddle we'll always stay two steps ahead o' em. *(Goes to the window, takes off his hat, and gazes out)* Phew. What a sight. Ain't seen anything like this since Mesquite Jenkins and me rode down to Lonetree Canyon some years ago

KIKI Mes-quite. Where he now?

YONG Last I heard, he was ambushed by some 'Paches. I'm sure most o' em was eatin' lead before they roped him up and took him away. Knowin' that sly ole son 'o a gun- he's still hauling his carcass around and is Chief Churupati The Second by now. But you never know with them 'Paches. They could be holding him up for a handsome sum of money. *(Pause)* Whew! one o' the slickest and fastest gunslingers you ever saw. Chalked up more 'n a few 'Paches in his day. Wouldn't draw with him even if his drinkin' lure me into it. Always can use a hombre like that to watch your backside.

KIKI Me. I your Mesquite Jenkins now.

YONG *(Chuckles)* Azalea, darlin', you 'bout the purtiest thing on two legs this side of the Peco's. And that weather-beaten hang-dog drifter 'bout as ugly as it gets. Ain't an inch of Mesquite Jenkins in you.

KIKI But I watch you back and you watch mine.

YONG Heh heh. Yes we'll watch each other's backs. But ain't much use watching my back if ya ain't much o' gunslinger, now is there? Not with all these Injuns about. *(Chuckles)* A man can lose more 'n just his life if his butt's not being closely watched.

KIKI You not love me.

YONG I didn't say that now.

KIKI Use me- only look, no touch-like trophy wife. *(Pause)* You not care for me.

YONG Sure I cares about you, but coverin' me during a crossfire ain't the same thing, now is it?

KIKI Azalea do anything for you.

YONG I know you would. But that ain't what we're talking about.

KIKI You not do same for Azalea.

YONG 'Course I would. *(Embraces her from behind)* Hell, nobody'd get within two miles of ya when I'm covering your cute behind.

KIKI *(Pushing him away)* No. You not love me.

YONG Well, I ain't too sure what you talkin' 'bout. All this ramblin' on 'bout "love". Only person I ever recall lovin' was my old lady. Besides, I can't be loving any ole two-legged creature who comes into my life, even if she does remind me of my mama and is as purty as you.

KIKI I knew. You not love me. *(Makes to leave)* Maybe I go back home.

YONG *(Stops her as she moves toward the door)* Don't get all teetered up on me now. I'm a cow-punchin' drifter. No drifter in his right mind sets in one place too long. Or with one woman. Now I ain't saying I love you, but I ain't never said I didn't. *(Pause)* You the first person that ever 'ppreciate who I really am. I knows that. Sure there were gals back at the bin who liked me, told me I was one 'o a kind, special and all that, but I never took to any one o' them. They were too strange for my tastes. Too much plump or too little class. But not you.

> *Disco ball comes on. Stars circle the walls and ceiling.*
> *The lights take on the pinkish hue of sunset.*

YONG Moment I laid eyes on you at the Chuckwagon, I knew you could understand who I was, that maybe for the first time in my life, I could hang my saddle and guns up for a gal. So here I am with you in some o' the roughest country I e'er seen and I'm looking toward that sunset because I plan on taking you there today. Now, that might not mean much to you, but it takes a lot for it to be coming outta my mouth. The sunset ain't a place you just take any ole gal. They gotta be special. They gotta be as purty as you are and glowing with that specialness on the inside. And if that don't mean much to ya, then, well, you can just go on.

> *Disco ball goes off. Lights return to normal.*

YONG *(Pointing to the door)* You just go on out there by your lonesome and just see what those Injuns are capable of. They'll eat ya alive and pick their teeth with yer bones. Any gal who has the mind of settin' off alone into 'Pache country ain't got enough birdfeed in her head to deserve a hombre like me. *(Pause)* Go on now. I ain't standin' in yer way. Git. *(Long pause)* Alright, then. Why don't you just sett' here for a moment and think 'bout what I just tell ya. I'll go an' just clear my mind and leave you in peace.

YONG *exits.*

KIKI *(Watching him leave, mutters)* No- please stay- I- I'm sorry. *(She falls to the floor, weeping)*

Fade out.
Lights come up slowly on the karaoke stage.
Spotlight on **YONG** *on stage ready to sing.*

D.J.'S VOICE Once again, ladies and gentlemen, here to sing that great song, "I Walk The Line", like no other singer can, let's hear it for our one and only, Karaoke Cowboy, Hop-a-long Cas-sidy.

The "APPLAUSE" sign blinks on and off.

D.J.'S VOICE Anybody in particular you'd like to send that song out to, Hoppy?

YONG *(Pointing to* **KIKI** *who is still on the floor, weeping)* Why, shore, to that lovely damsel sitting right over there.

Disco ball goes on. Stars circle the walls and ceiling.
KIKI *begins to rise slowly, watching him as he begins his song.*

YONG *(Sings Johnny Cash's "I Walk The Line")*
I keep a close watch on this heart of mine.
I keep my eyes wide open all the time.
I keep the ends all tied up till it's fine.
Because you're mine, I walk the line.

I find it very very easy to be true.
I find myself alone when each day's through.
Yes, I'll admit that I'm a fool for you.

Because you're mine, I walk the line.
As sure as night is dark and day is light.
I keep you on my mind both day and night.
Any happiness I've known proves that it's right.
Because you're mine, I walk the line.

You've got a way to keep me on your side.
You give me cause for love that I can't hide.
For you I know I'd even try to turn the tide.
Because you're mine, I walk the line.

I keep a close watch on this heart of mine.
I keep my eyes wide open all the time.
I keep the ends all tied up till it's fine.
Because you're mine, I walk the line.

Disco ball goes off.
Lights slowly fade out on the karaoke stage. **YONG** *exits.*
The "APPLAUSE" sign blinks on and off.

KIKI *(To the audience)* These days things get better for me-- feeling more center than when I first come to this country. First there was the Terror-- that black hole-- a new culture-- new language-- I am alone-- cut off-- no belonging-- no connection. Back home when I feel lonely-- I hide from others—even though they still part of me. But here-- opposite happen-- when I feel lonely, I go to *them*-- to others-- for comfort-- long nights at coffee shop—or karaoke bar-- with fellow visa student-- talk about times when the other people were, well, just like us. *(Pause)* I missed that feeling. So cannot fall sleep-- cannot wake up-- cannot go class-- cannot do anything-- so hang out all day-- all night-- in Little Tokyo-- this small town in small city-- by time you say "hello"-- already pass through Italy to Korea-- from Rome to Seoul in two syllable. This place so proud be real thing-- real Japanese food-- real Japanese people-- so real not even Japanese feel at home. *(Pause)* So then-- it all come to me-- all at once it come-- like walking into wall—the-- the unrealness of this place-- of everything-- I am ghost-- forever I wander-- a town made of cardboard boxes-- like John Wayne movie.

(Pause) I need get out-- not want to live like ghost-- no more-- to be alive-- live-- be whole again! *(Pause)* But always problem living in this country-- no real center-- in Japan you never think about-- never question yourself-- here everything always moving under your feet-- like earthshake-- one moment you know where you standing-- who you are-- where you come from-- then next moment you don't know-- second guessing-- always second guessing. My friends at home would not like here-- like my man say-- like walking line-- tight line-- you always be walking line if you are a person like me-- if you are on one side, then people on other side make fun of you-- put you down-- think you play for wrong team. *(In Japanese, parodying an older Japanese woman)* "If you're from Japan, you should speak Japanese." *(In English. To the audience)* Why I speak Japanese when I come here to learn English? Then I am with friends in Tim Horton's-- speaking Japanese-- some white woman say "Go back to your own country if you can't speak our language." Very confusing-- nobody know where they are-- which side of line they standing-- only confused people on both side telling you who you are not. *(Pause)* So, that night-- when he sing me song-- dedicate-- to *me*-- nobody else-- feel light again-- like dancing with angel-- like old self died-- went to heaven.

YONG *enters, sits in* **JAMES'** *former place.*

KIKI Later—after song—he come sit with me—at my table—seem sad—so I ask him if something wrong.

YONG Nothin' darling, nothin'…

KIKI But I keep pushing him—to talk to me.

YONG Haven't been myself these days. I'm…I'm sorry Azalea.

KIKI You fine—sing beautiful

YONG Why thank you. You're sweeter than home-made apple pie. It's not that. It's not the singing. It's that sometimes I get a bit mixed up. Don't knows who I am in this city anymore. Can be confusin'

sometimes with everything happenin' so quickly around you. I reckon it's time to be moseying on out of here soon. Pack up the saddlebags and git on out.

KIKI Yes, yes. You take Azalea.

YONG Don't know why people are so stuck in their ways. Lookin' through horse blinders. Can't see either way but…*(Gestures by putting both hands by his eyes)*…like this. Thinkin' they got it all figured out. Life should be much simpler, like the old days when all you had was a cattle outfit in a wild country with just the open sky to keep you company. It can be a hard, lonely life, but a rewarding one. These days, nothin' is so simple. Everybody runnin' around trying to rustle together some coin, but they forget why they're here, forget what they're runnin' around for in the first place.

KIKI You great as you are.

YONG I thank you, darlin', but…I dunno. Don't you ever wonder what this is all about?

KIKI Yes, always think about.

YONG Hell, I dunno what I'm talking about. Ramblin' on like this. You're a mighty nice girl. Don't find too many out here in the city. *(Pause)* Don't mind me. I'm jus' ramblin', I guess, that's all.

Lights fade to black.

Lights up on the **SHERIFF**.

SHERIFF Well, now that I think about it, I got the call approximately seventeen-hundred hours and twelve minutes to be precise. I have to tell you, and it's the God's honest truth, I never would have believed it if I didn't hear it coming outta that telephone and into my own ear. Now, this here is a small town, so tiny that it says "Welcome" on both sides of the sign. Population of approximately one-thousand, three-hundred and nine men, women, and children to be precise. *(Beat)* You see, the ranch is for tourists coming up from the city for the weekend. Or sometimes hospitals for the mentally-challenged like the one that come up that day. A field trip for their patients. Get some country air into their heads. There are no more than five or six Shetland ponies, so they don't antici…antici…they don't expect much business to begin with. So when Murdock called to tell me that someone had run off with his prize Shetland, Barney, well, I couldn't believe it. I immediately thought it was one of them Indians from the Rez pulling a prank, but when he said it was some Chinese, I thought "hell, what is Mr. Fong doing leaving his restaurant and stealing horses for?" Then Murdock tell me that it wasn't Mr. Fong or his wife. It was a coupla Chinese from the mental hospital. So I asked Shackup Charlotte if she'd seen anybody on her way into work. She does the night shift at the jailhouse. And she'd said that she had, but didn't think nothing of it. Just some tourists working the trail on a pony, is what she said.

"Which direction did they head," I asked her.

"Toward Loon Lake, on this side of the rez" she said.

"There ain't nothing there except for O'Connor's old cabin," I said. "Maybe I'll go and check it out."

"You want me to come with you, Sheriff?" she said.

Charlotte got this thing for putting handcuffs on folks, you see.

"No, you stay here and man the phones."

So, anyways, I must have taken two steps down from the jailhouse when I see a strange apparition coming down the street. It was one of them Indian boys on one of Murdock's ponies riding straight through town, down Main Street, here. The poor kid was facing backwards and holdin' onto its tail. And that's when I knew somethin' really fishy was going on. So I rushed out there toward the lake, approximately seventeen-hundred hours and forty-seven minutes to be precise.

Blackout.

Sound of a horse's whinny offstage.
Lights up on the cabin.
YONG *rushes in.*
He gestures at **KIKI** *to hide.* **KIKI** *pulls a blanket over herself on the floor.*

A couple of drunken voices are heard outside.
YONG *goes to the side of the door and takes a peek outside. He stands ready, gun in his hand.*
JONAH *and* **LOUIS** *enter, cautiously at first, peering their heads past the black bear rug hanging over the doorframe.*
JONAH *is holding a bottle of Jack Daniels in a brown paper bag.*
Both are slightly intoxicated.

LOUIS What'd I tell 'ya, you fool. Nobody here. The place is as empty as your head. *(Pause. Referring to the black bear rug hanging over the door)* Funny. I don't remember hanging that thing there.

JONAH I swear to Manitou that I saw somebody run in here, Louis.

LOUIS You're just seeing things again. If that somebody's around, he'll have put a gun to your head by now.

JONAH But what about Murdock's pony that's-

YONG *(Pointing the gun at* **JONAH'S** *temple)* Put your hands up very, very slowly.

LOUIS What da...?

JONAH What I'd tell ya, Louis.

YONG *(Pointing the gun now at* **JONAH'S** *mouth)* Put your hands up, else you'll be eating some lead.

They slowly put their hands up.

LOUIS Look sir, you take it easy, we're not meaning any harm.

JONAH Yeah, we didn't come to crash no party or nothing, eh?

LOUIS What are you anyway, the authorities or something?

YONG *(Holding the gun under **LOUIS'** chin)* No, I'm jus' the meanest hombre you'll ever meet…and mebbe the last.

JONAH Then you couldn't be the law. Our Sheriff is the wimpiest geek-

LOUIS Shut the hell up, will ya? Let me handle this.

YONG Who are you? And what d'ya want here?

JONAH I'm Jonah Beavertooth Napoleon the Third and this here friend of mine is Louis Long Lance for reasons I can't share with you. We just come- like we do every Saturday- to drink up before heading off to the Thunder Cove Palace. Isn't that right, Louis?

LOUIS What did I tell you about keeping your trap shut?

YONG 'Paches. Just as I thought.

JONAH Apaches? Apaches! We ain't no Apaches. *(Pause)* Are we, Louis?

LOUIS Cree. We're Cree, you fool. *(Attempts a mixed up version of high-brow English)* And who might we have the pleasure of your company?

JONAH Yeah, who the hell you think you are, eh?

> **LOUIS** *glares at* **JONAH**.

JONAH Shutting it. I'm shutting it, Louis.

LOUIS *(High-brow English)* You'll have to excuse my compatriot. He knows not what I speak.

YONG What happened to my amigo?

LOUIS And who might you be referring to when you refer to the reference of "amigo"?

YONG Mesquite Jenkins.

JONAH Mosquito who?

YONG Mes-quite Jen-kins. You know who I'm talking about. Don't you play stupid with me.

LOUIS Mister, we're just a coupl 'a poor Indians from the rez comin' here for a good time. We'll be on our way.

JONAH: Yeah, we come 'round here every Saturday Night before the bingo-

KIKI *(Coming out from under the blanket)* Bingo! "A popular gambling game with cards divided into numbered squares." Bingo! BINGO!

JONAH Yeah, yeah. Bingo! BINGO! *(Pause)* Hey, who are you? Where'd you all of a sudden come from anyway?

KIKI Saitama.

JONAH Sai-what?

KIKI Saitama. Japan.

JONAH Is that how they say "from under a blanket" in Chinamen's language, Louis?

LOUIS *(To JONAH)* Sa-ee-ta-ma, you fool! Don't you know your geology?

JONAH Oh, right, of course. Sa-ee-ta-ma. I think I remember now...

YONG Now, let's get back to the bizness here. You gonna tell me where you hid Mesquite Jenkins or am I gonna have to pump you full 'o lead to get you to talk.

LOUIS Now, just one second, Mister, uh…

YONG Cassidy.

LOUIS Mister Cassidy. I don't know what happened to this friend of yours…

YONG Mesquite Jenkins.

LOUIS Right, him. But I know that neither me nor my friend had anything to do with his tragic disappearance. Me and Jonah here-

JONAH *(Proudly)* Jonah Beavertooth Napoleon The Third.

> *Pause*

LOUIS I don't know anything about your friend, but maybe if we sat down like the men that we are and discussed this over…*(Grabs the paper bag from* **JONAH** *and holds it out to* **YONG***)*…this here relaxative, Jonah and I might be of some assistance.

JONAH Yeah, I'm getting thirsty with all this gunslinging cowboys and indians stuff.

YONG *(To* **JONAH***, pointing a gun to his head)* I ain't in the mood for fooling with you, boy.

LOUIS *(Intervening on* **JONAH'S** *behalf, with a nervous chuckle. Shoves the paper bag back to him)* Don't mind him. He's just being himself Mister Cassidy. *(To* **JONAH***)* Now, apologize to the man before he pumps ya full of lead. Show the man some respect!

JONAH I'm sorry, Mister Cassidy. With that fine gun you got there, and your lovely outfit, you deserve all the respect in the world. *(Imitating Clint Eastwood's Dirty Harry)* "Go ahead, make my day." *(Bursts out spontaneously into a nervous laugh)*

LOUIS *elbows* **JONAH** *in the stomach.*

JONAH Owwww! Why'd you do that for?

LOUIS Just trying to save your damn life, that's all. With your mouth babbling like a brook, you're liable to get us both killed. *(To* **YONG***)* Mister Cassidy, now that I think about it, I do know who you're talking about. This…this…

YONG Mesquite Jenkins.

LOUIS *(At the same time)* Mesquite Jenkins…fellow. You see, the Apaches sold him to us for some…beaver pelts.

YONG *(Places his gun on the table and scratches his head)* 'Paches sold him to ya, did they? Just as I thought…

   JONAH *gives* **LOUIS** *a look of confusion.*

LOUIS Why shore. *(Inconspicuously walks past* **YONG** *toward the table. To* **KIKI***, taking off his Toronto Maple Leafs cap)* Evening, ma'am. You're a very pretty woman. Ain't she, Jonah? *(Signals* **JONAH** *to come over toward the table)*

JONAH She shore is.

KIKI *(Blushing. To* **LOUIS***, with a Scarlett O'hara twang to her voice)* Why, thank you kindly, Mr… *(Reaching out to shake his hand)*

LOUIS *(Confused, he stops reaching for the other gun on the table and shakes her hand)* Long Lance. Named after the great Canadian movie star, Long Lance Silver. The pride and glory of our people, ain't that so Jonah?

JONAH That's right. Just like Napoleon. He was a hero, too. My grammy named me after him because I was born small, but she knew I would do big things.

KIKI Napoleon. Nap-o-leon.

JONAH That's my name, don't wear it out.

LOUIS *(Attempting to distract her)* She's so damn pretty, don't think I've seen anybody as pretty as her in all my life.

> **KIKI** *turns away, embarrassed.*
> **YONG** *whips around, pointing the other gun in his hand in the general vicinity of the table.*
> **LOUIS** *pulls his hand away quickly.*
> **YONG** *doesn't see this.*

YONG Now, what was this about some beaver pelts?

LOUIS Yes…the beaver pelts. Well, eh hem, it goes like this. The Cree and the Apaches have this trade agreement, you see.

JONAH We do?

LOUIS *(Gives **JONAH** another elbow. **JONAH** bowls over in pain)* And what this trade agreement stipulates is that for every white man caught- your friend is white, isn't he?

YONG Who Mesquite?

LOUIS Well, what I mean by white, of course, is that it covers a whole range of colours including black and brown and yellow, really…

YONG Mesquite Jenkins, hell, he's as white as a lily-livered hangdog.

LOUIS Exactly. So for every lily-livered white man that is caught, you see, we give the Apaches five beaver pelts in exchange.

YONG Just five pelts, huh?

LOUIS Well, the exchange rate, you know. Too unpredictable these days.

YONG Go on. Where is he now, then?

LOUIS Well, he's over…on the Reserve tending to some buffalo on Old Chancey Eli's…buffalo ranch.

JONAH I never knew Old Chancey Eli had a buffalo range?

> **JONAH** *realizes what he has done wrong, elbows himself in the side and bowls over in pain again.*

KIKI Why he keep do this?

LOUIS For interrupting me so much, Ma'am. You see, when he interrupts me, his body goes into a fit just like that. *(To **JONAH**)* Now looka here, Jonah, can't you see I'm trying to help here Mister Cassidy get to the bottom of all this and find what he's come here lookin' for?

> **YONG** *swivels around and looks out the door. He is downright confused by the new set of circumstances his friend, Mesquite Jenkins, is in.*
> **KIKI** *watches him with concern.*
> *The following series of actions unfolds in slow motion.*
> **LOUIS** *reaches out for the gun on the table, grabs it, and takes cover behind*
> **KIKI**, *holding her against him with one arm while pointing the gun at*
> **YONG'S** *back with the other.*
> *A sound comes out of **KIKI'S** mouth, which is immediately stifled by*
> **LOUIS'** *hand.*
> **YONG** *swings around, his gun already drawn and ready to fire.*
> *There is a long tense silence that fills the room.*
> *In regular speed,* **JONAH**, *sitting under the table, his knees buckling underneath him, takes a long swig from the paper bag.*

YONG You'd let go of her if you knew what's good for ya. I'm the fastest shot this side of the Pecos. *(Slowly)* Let…her…go.

LOUIS I don't know what kind of Fu Man Chu's Wild West Show dumped you off in this here town, Mister Cas-s-idy, but you better hope the two o' ya's get back to it alive. *(Pointing the gun to* **KIKI'S** *temple)* Now, you might have the fastest shot on this side of whatever, but I'm not looking to miss either when I pull this trigger. So if I were you, I'd drop it very slowly from where you're standing if you ever want to see your girl's head here in one pretty piece. *(Pause.* **YONG** *glares at* **LOUIS***, holding it for a few beats)* I'm counting to three. And on the count of three, I want to see that dangerous toy in your hand ease gently to the floor. *(Pause)* One…Two…Three! *(***LOUIS** *cocks the trigger on the gun. Momentarily confused)* Alright, then, four…five…six! *(On the cusp of firing the gun,* **YONG** *slowly bends forward and gently lays the gun on the floor)* Alright, cowboy, easy does it. Now, put your hands on your head and get on your knees.

YONG *doesn't budge.*

LOUIS What the hell is the matter with you, you fuckin' Chinaman, can't you understand no english? You heard what I said! Put your goddamn hand on your fuckin' hat!! *(He jostles* **KIKI** *who whimpers)*

YONG Now take it easy on the gal, Amigo.

LOUIS I'm not you're fuckin' amigo, partner. What do you think this is, some Cheech and Chong flick? Now do like I tell ya and put your hands on top of your head, real slow. *(***YONG** *slowly puts his hands on his hat)* Alright. Now. *(Calling to* **JONAH***)* Jonah. *(***JONAH** *is muttering, his knees shaking like leaves)* JONAH!

JONAH Oh Christ, oh Christ…Don't shoot, please don't shoot me.

LOUIS JONAH! Get your ass over here.

JONAH *(Crawls out from under the table and goes toward* **LOUIS***, arms extended and eyes still closed)* Yes, Louis, yes, yes… *(Bumps into a chair)* Oh my god, Oh my god.

LOUIS Open your eyes, you fool!

JONAH opens his eyes. He can't believe what he's seeing: the tables have been turned. He rushes over to LOUIS and embraces him.

JONAH You're alive, Louis Long Lance. Thank god you're alive!

LOUIS Get offa me, you goddamn fool and go get the gun.

JONAH What gun? Where?

LOUIS On the floor, in front of that slant-eyed John Wayne over there.

JONAH hesitates.

LOUIS Go pick up the gun!

JONAH rushes over picks up the gun, juggles it in his hands as if he was holding a hot potato. He brings it over to LOUIS and steps aside. LOUIS points both guns now at YONG.

LOUIS Now, cowboy, get down on the floor. (Pause) MOVE IT!

YONG gets down on the floor, hands still on his head.

LOUIS Jonah.

JONAH Yes, Louis.

LOUIS (Eyeing **YONG** the whole time) I want you to go out that door, get on that horse out there, ride down into town and get the Sheriff.

JONAH But you know I don't ride ponies.

YONG If Topper ever lets you get on him, he won't ever let you get off.

LOUIS (To **YONG**) You keep your trap shut. I'm running the show here. (To **JONAH**) Now just do as I say!

JONAH But...but...

LOUIS *(Waves the gun in the direction of* **JONAH***)* Get going! Or else I'll have to shoot all of ya and get the Sheriff myself.

> **JONAH** *rushes out past* **YONG***.*
> *There is the sound of the horse whinnying, resisting as* **JONAH** *tries to get on its saddle.*

JONAH Nice horsey horsey. Good boy.

> *After a few moments of struggling with the horse, there is the sound of the horse clopping away from the cabin, followed by the sound of* **JONAH** *hollering with terror.*
> *Lights slowly begin to fade.*

LOUIS *(Pointing a gun at both* **YONG** *and* **KIKI***. He proceeds toward* **YONG***)* Now, you wanna play cowboys and indians, do ya?

Blackout.

Spotlight on **LOUIS***, facing the audience.*

LOUIS First things first. I won't deny it. The picture in the weekly Loon Lake Dispatch didn't lie. Sure, Jonah was caught riding backwards through town, but you have to remember he always was a bit scared of horses. Never liked sitting on one. He was also a bit tipsy when I sent him to get the Sheriff. *(Beat)* I'm sure he's sobered up by now. Guess we won't know till they find him. *(Pause)* Anyways back to the testimony. If you're asking me, I think that cowboy was a good man. Good character. A bit confused, but who isn't nowadays? Even I forget sometimes that I'm a Cree belonging to the Loon Lake band. It's easy to forget when you got images plastered all over the place telling you who you are. Ever since you White folks came here, I've been given so many different identities I can't even remember half of them. These days we are the Lazy Ones, Drunks, Glue-Sniffers, Wife-Beaters, Barricade-Makers, Homeless, Jobless. The list is endless. Sure, I know most of you hold second thoughts about all that. Second-guessing what the schools and churches and newspapers and movies and books and Grey Owl and Pocahontas, keep telling you we are. You're complicated folks. I understand. Lookit, I'm not saying all the images of Indian life are bad. For example, do this exercise tonight. When you go home, ask your child to draw you a picture of an Indian. *(Pause)* See, we're making progress. *(Pause)* Right, back to the cowboy. There is one thing I can say about him. He knew how real us Indians were. There was respect there. Never a moment when he took me or Jonah for granted. Real respect. And about the girl, he had lots of love for her, too. I could tell. He woulda given his life for her. Lots of love there. *(Pause)* He was an authentic cowboy. The real thing. There aren't too many cowboys like him around these days. In a place like this, a cowboy like that has the deck stacked against him. *(Pause)* I kinda miss him actually.

Blackout.

Karaoke Bar.

YONG *stands on the platform. The disk jockey's voice comes over the speakers- garbled and dreamy, as if he was speaking loudly in slow motion.*

D.J.'S VOICE Foooor thhhhe laaast tiiiimmmme tooonieeeght, lettttts welcooooome baaaack too thhhe stayyyyyge, hhhhour frrrreeeennnd, Hooooopaloonnng Caaaassssidy.

YONG *Sings Hank Williams' "Kaw-Liga"*
Kaw-Liga was a wooden Indian standing by the door.
He fell in love with an Indian maid over in the antique store.
Kaw-Liga...
Just stood there and never let it show,
So she could never answer "yes" or "no".

He always wore his Sunday feathers and held a tomahawk.
The maiden wore her beads and braids and hoped someday he'd talk.
Kaw-Liga...
Too stubborn to ever show a sign

Because his heart was made of knotty pine.
Poor old Kaw-Liga he never got a kiss.
Poor old Kaw-Liga he don't know what he missed.
Is it any wonder that his face is red.
Kaw-Liga that poor old wooden head.

Kaw-Liga was a lonely Indian, never went nowhere.
His heart would sit on the Indian maid with the cold black hair.
Kaw-Liga…
Just stood there and never let it show,
So she could never answer "yes" or "no".

And then one day a wealthy customer bought the Indian maid.
And took her oh so far away but Old Kaw-Liga stayed.
Kaw-Liga…
Just standing there as lonely as can be
And wishes he was still an old pine-tree.

Poor old Kaw-Liga he never got a kiss.
Poor old Kaw-Liga he don't know what he missed.
Is it any wonder that his face is red.
Kaw-Liga that poor old wooden head.

A spotlight dimly on **KIKI**.
LOUIS *is frozen in tableau.*
KIKI *turns her head to face the audience, her body still being held by*
LOUIS.

KIKI   One day Yong take me to his home-- to the Bin he used to call it-- nurses and doctors everywhere-- poking at everyone who look like they dead. *(Pause. Sighs)* Happy times-- sit in Rec room all day-- play cards—checkers-- learn the tricks of trade-- like what Mesquite Jenkins teach him when they pass through town together-- try to find job-- then he teach to me-- so good now. So good at it that he say…*(Imitating* **YONG**)…"better 'n any driftin' cowpuncher who's ever dropped a nickel in his life." *(Pause)* On weekend he get a pass-- free to go anywhere-- we sit in park-- he play guitar-- such sad song he learn on frontier-- learn by himself-- one he used to always play-- a song to end all song. With this song, no more Karaoke-- hang up microphone once and for all-- this song for keeps-- no more imitate other people voices-- singing their songs-- pretend be someone else. He wrote himself-- nobody sing for him-- too close to his heart, he say. I forget now how it goes, but about find some peace-- like when you have bad time-- need a break-- this was about all that-- going through so much pain-- yes, one break or two in life not bad thing. *(Pause)* No, not bad thing at all.

Fade out.

The cabin.
YONG, **LOUIS**, *and* **KIKI** *break out of their tableau.*

LOUIS *(Rising. Pointing a gun at both* **YONG** *and* **KIKI**. *He proceeds toward* **YONG***)* Now, you wanna play cowboys and indians, do ya? *(Pause)* I'll show you cowboys and indians. *(To* **YONG***, standing over him)* Get up! I said get up! *(To* **KIKI***)* …and you stay down. *(***YONG** *rises slowly from off the floor)* So you think you're a cowboy, eh? A chinaman cowboy. Funniest thing I ever seen. You should be delivering Mr. Fong's Chinese food for him. You'd make a good tip. *(Flicks* **YONG'S** *hat off with the barrel of his gun)* Okay, now I'm gonna show you how you really play cowboys and indians. *(Goes around* **YONG***, still pointing the gun at him, and picks up the hat. He puts it on his head. Affects a cowboy twang to his voice)* Well, hot-diggity-dawg, I'll be goddamned. *(Posing in a draw stance)* Am I the wildest-shooting gunfighter in the West or what? *(To* **KIKI***)* What d'ya think, doll. *(Posing for her)* Is this be-coming on me?

KIKI *(Gazing into space as if in deep thought)* Be-coming. "To come into being." Becoming.

LOUIS That's right, honey, you just stay in that comfort zone o' yours. I got biz'ness to take care of. *(To himself)* Fuckin' nutbar. *(Goes to* **YONG** *and gestures to the holster with a gun)* That's right, hand 'em over. Ya can't be a cowboy without one of 'em, now can you? *(***YONG** *doesn't budge)* What's the matter, boy, 'fraid your damsel here will look at you another way without yer gun drawers?

(He laughs. Seriously, now, waving the gun) Now take 'em off.

YONG *takes them off. Holster drops to the floor.*

YONG I'll get you yet, you rattlesnake.

LOUIS *(Circles around* **YONG***)* I'm a rattlesnake now, am I? First I'm an Apache, now I'm a rattlesnake. If I'm a rattlsnake…*(Closes in on* **YONG***. Puts the barrel of the gun to* **YONG'S** *temple)* …why, then, you ain't nothin' but a hounddog. *(He moves away, laughing)* Now toss that thing over. (**YONG** *walks out of the holster, picks it up, and tosses it to* **LOUIS**. **LOUIS** *straps it on, slides the guns in. Imitating John Wayne)* "Why this ole pile o' logs ain't big enough for the two of us, partner." *(He draws, fumbling as he twirls the guns on his fingers. Pointing the guns at* **YONG***)* BANG! BANG! (**KIKI** *cowers under the blanket. To* **YONG***)* Scared ya, didn't I? Go on, tell me I scared ya. Tell me. *(Pointing the gun at* **KIKI***)* TELL ME I SCARED YA!!

YONG *(Almost inaudibly)* You…you scared me.

LOUIS I can't hear you, cowboy. Speak up.

YONG *(Louder, but still nearly a whisper)* You scared me.

LOUIS Cat got your tongue, boy? Or did you eat the cat before it could? *(Beat)* Or maybe, just maybe, you don't give two shits about your damsel's life. *(He cocks the gun pointed at* **KIKI***)*

YONG YOU SCARED ME! YOU SCARED ME!! (**KIKI** *begins to cry)* Now, tell me what you want. You're scarin' the gal.

LOUIS What do I want? What do I want? You break into our little hang-out, me and Jonah's, take us hostage, and you want to know what I want? *(Beat)* Why you got some nerve, mister. You want to know what I want? I'll tell you what I fuckin' want! *(Pause)* I want you to dance.

YONG What…?

LOUIS To dance. You heard me. Never been asked to dance before? *(Walks across the room toward the fireplace. He unhooks one of the Indian headdresses. Turns around quickly and tosses it to* **YONG***, who catches it)* Now put it on. *(***YONG** *doesn't budge)* Is it me? Am I speaking to myself or are all you chinamen cowboys born deaf-mute? *(***YONG** *puts it on)* I stand corrected. I was wrong if Nanabush be my witness. You're a chinaman cowboy who *can* hear. Hallelujah! *(Takes the black bear rug from off the door frame) (To* **KIKI***)* And you, get up!

KIKI Me…?

LOUIS Yeah, you. What's your name, by the way, sweet darlin'.

KIKI Azalea.

LOUIS Azalea. That's real cute. Cute name to match a cute face. What d'ya done to your face there, Azalea? Don't you know how put all that mascara and stuff on right? *(For a moment,* **KIKI** *feels self-conscious about her appearance.* **LOUIS** *goes over to* **KIKI** *and hands the bear rug to her)* I know a good manu-curist back at the reserve. Her name is Grin-toothed Phoenix Leveecrag. Fix you up real good for real cheap.
(Beat) Never mind. Back to the biz-ness at hand. Put it on. *(Goes to* **KIKI** *and arranges the bear's headpiece over her head)* Now, don't be touching it. Just leave it as it is. Looks good on ya. *(A grandiose pause as he looks over the spectacle)* So. We ready? *(No response)* Good. This is what you call a "War Dance". *(To* **KIKI***)* You see any Westerns back in your homeland, Azalea? *(***KIKI** *nods enthusiastically)* Good. Then you know what a "War Dance", right? *(***KIKI** *shakes her head)* Ya see, before the Injuns go to war 'gainst the white folks who been pillagin' their land and raping their women, they do this little dance, see? *(Pause)* Hold on a second here. We're missing something. *(Looks around the cabin. Sees a couple of objects.* **KIKI** *looks pleadingly over at* **YONG***, who turns his head away from her in shame. To* **KIKI***, handing her a large soup ladle and a tin frying pan)* Here, you hold onto this. *(To* **YONG***, handing him a long scraggly leafless branch.* **YONG** *takes it grudgingly)* Don't get all tem-per-mental on me now. *(He takes a step back from the scene, looks it over, takes the blanket from* **KIKI***, bundles it up on the floor, in front of the chesterfield. Pointing to the blanket)* That's a fire.

KIKI Not fire. Blanket.

LOUIS I know that's a blanket, darlin'. You think I'm stupid or something? Ever hear of a metaphor. An imitation of something?

KIKI Immigration. Foreigners entering a country to marry a citizen and seek permanent residence status. Immigration.

LOUIS Not immi-gration, darlin', Imi-tation. Never mind. You just use your *Immi-gration*, honey, and pretend that that blanket is a campfire. Can ya do that for me? (**KIKI** *nods her head*) Alright, then. (*Pause*) Okey-dokey. Now. Like I was saying, a "War Dance" is something the Indians did before they went out to slaughter the white man and scalp their heads off. You seen the movies. So what I want you to do is pretend you're going to kill the white folk tomorrow morning before the sun rises and dance like it's the last dance you'll ever have. (*Pause*) Okay, begin. (*Nobody moves*) You can't dance if you're just standing still in one spot, now, can ya? (*To* **KIKI**) Start hitting that frying pan with the spoon. (**KIKI** *hits it once*) Good. Now keep hitting it. Don't get all timid on me now. (**KIKI** *keeps hitting the pan, irrhythmically*) Good. Good. Just like that. Keep hitting it. (**KIKI** *continues to hit the pan, seeming to enjoy it*) Now, I want you to lift your feet up and down like somebody lit a fire under your feet. (**KIKI** *lifts her legs up and down as if she was walking on the spot*) Good, now just a bit quicker, darlin'. (**KIKI** *moves quicker, trying to co-ordinate her banging with her leg movement*) Beautiful, beautiful. (*Turns to* **YONG**) Now, you, cowboy. Do what she's doing, except bend your body up and down with your legs. (**YONG** *doesn't move. There is a steely hate exuding from him.* **LOUIS** *cocks the trigger on one of the guns*) You ain't as good a listener as your damsel here. Is it my instructions you don't comper-hend or just the english? (*Imitating an Englishman*) Perhaps my English isn't quite to your satisfaction, old chap? (*Seriously*) Now, move. (**YONG** *begins to move, very awkwardly. To* **KIKI**) Keep it up, doll. That's good. Now, as you do that, walk around that fire- that blanket- for me. (**KIKI** *does this. To* **YONG**) Follow her around the fire, but start moving that spear- the branch in your hand- like this. (*He illustrates this by extending his right arm and bending back and forth from the elbow.* **KIKI** *bumps into* **YONG**. *To* **YONG**)

You got to keep moving. *(They both start moving in unison, fumbling over their own feet, but keeping to the general spirit of what was instructed)* Now, start chanting. (**KIKI** *and* **YONG** *stop in their tracks, confused)* Don't stop, keep going, but I want you to start chanting like this. *(He illustrates by making a noise, while pressing the palm of his hand to his mouth and releasing it very quickly. This is your stereotype Comanche Indian war chant you pick up in the Hollywood Western movies)* Yai-yai-yai…yai-yai-yai…yai-yai-yai… *(He stands back as* **YONG** *and* **KIKI** *perform a grotesque version of an Indian War Dance. He is entranced by this. The "War Dance" goes on for a few minutes. Muttering)* Beautiful…beautiful.

> *Suddenly, somebody enters quickly through the door. It is the* **SHERIFF**, *his gun already drawn and ready to fire.*

SHERIFF FREEZE EVERYBODY! LOUIS LONG LANCE, DROP YOUR GUN!

> *Startled,* **LOUIS** *drops his guns to the floor.*
> **YONG** *rushes for the guns before the* **SHERIFF** *can even blink, picks them up, and cross-points one at* **LOUIS**, *who has now retreated to a corner, and the other at the* **SHERIFF**, *who follows* **YONG** *with his own gun.*
> **KIKI** *cowers to the floor.*
> *All actions happen in slow motion.*
> **LOUIS** *waves his arms over his face and opens his mouth to say something.*
> **SHERIFF** *waves his free hand up and down, also opening his mouth to say something.*
> **KIKI**, *reaching out for* **YONG'S** *leg, also opens her mouth to say something.*
> **YONG'S** *guns fire first, two shots, but instead of bullets, two white flags pop out of the barrels with the word "BANG!" written on it.*
> *Almost at the same instant, the* **SHERIFF** *fires a shot, the smoke coming out of the end of the barrel.*
> *All actions return to normal speed.*
> **YONG** *crumples forward to the floor.*

LOUIS Oh, my god…oh, my god…

BALLAD OF A KARAOKE COWBOY

SHERIFF *looks over the scene, shocked at what he has done.*
KIKI *rises slowly from her position and walks over to* **YONG'S** *fallen body like a ghost.*
She drops herself onto her knees and cradles **YONG'S** *head in her lap. There is blood everywhere; a bright thick pool on the floor around him, soaked deeply into his shirt and squirting between his fingers from his stomach. The blood should continue to flow through the rest of the scene, a grisly sight.*

YONG *(On the floor squirming in pain)* I'm shot…he shot me. *(Laughs)* In the stomach…dangerous. *(Pause)* He…he gunned me down. *(To the* **SHERIFF***)* You, you…shot me…LOOK AT WHAT YOU DID! YOU SHOT ME!

SHERIFF *(Lamely)* …you drew first…

YONG *(Pause. Spitting blood from his mouth)* Oh, gawd… *(To* **KIKI***)* I'm not supposed to die like this…Not like this… *(To* **KIKI***)* I always got out of this- always. The worst-- been through the worst. Ask Mesquite…Jenkins yerself. He was there-- always there-- by my side—saved my life more than a few times. *(Pause)*…you're my Mesquite Jenkins now…*(Gasping for breath. To* **KIKI***)* You're so beautiful…so beautiful…*(Pause)* I'm scared baby-- scared-- so scared… *(Coughs up more blood)* Last night—back at the bin— the nurses let me out—I was waiting for you to visit—so there I was in the yard-- the moon was long gone—when I looked up at the sky-- I swear I could see every star in the universe—huddlin' together in that small patch of darkness between the buildings—a square pond of stars straight above my head—I, uh, I thought to myself-- "Shore is beautiful up there. Wish my Azalea was here beside me to-- to watch this with me." There was this one star—it was a big one-- blazing across this square pond-- bursting into a fireball and-- and just like that-- gone-- suddenly, gone, disappeared into the pond—like a fish jumping out of water and back in agin-- wondered mebbe we are all like that-- that star-- one big burst of light before goin' agin-- Gone for good-- I don't know-- makes you feel kinda small when you think about it-- all them stars up there. Each one o' them a billion years old-- some the size of ten thousand planet earths. Makes you feel kinda small-- Gawd, when you

43

think about a thing like that. *(Coughs. Lights begin to change into a pinkish hue, the colour of sunset)* Who's going—who's going to-- take care of you-- take you out there?

The lead in to the next song begins to come up, slowly, quietly.

KIKI You. Only you.

YONG *(To **KIKI**)* Yes…only me…of course. *(Pause)* I've always… loved you, Azalea. You knew me…you were my…only friend…

KIKI Yes.

YONG …I'm sorry 'bout this…don't want to leave you alone…don't want you to feel lonely…*(To **LOUIS**)* Come here. *(**LOUIS** crawls over to him, bawling his eyes, and bends over)* Take care of her…she's a good girl.

LOUIS I will.

YONG …you promise me, you hear?…

LOUIS I…I promise.

YONG *(Turns to the **SHERIFF**)* …Not your fault, Sheriff… I drew first…

He goes unconscious.

KIKI *(Shaking him)* Hoppy! Wake up. *(Pause)* Hoppy. Please. Don't go. *(**LOUIS** tries to lift her to her feet)* No.

LOUIS Come on, lady, let's go. He's dead.

KIKI NO! *(Beat)* NO! NO!! *(Screaming)* NOOOOOOOO…!!!

Blackout.
*A spotlight comes on blindingly over **YONG**.*

He writhes on the floor ever so slightly, the pool of blood beginning to grow around him.
His last few moments before death.
The disco ball goes on. Stars circle the walls and ceilings.
KIKI *enters onto the singing stage.*
The lead in to the song comes up over the speakers.
Over the course of the song, the spotlight on **YONG** *dims, up until the last convulsion and gasp for breath. The song should end with his last breath and the spotlight goes to black.*
LOUIS *is sitting at the karaoke table, wearing a cowboy hat, and watching* **KIKI**.

KIKI   *(Speaking over the lead into the song. With a "country" twang to her voice)* I'd like to dedicate this ballad to all you cowboys out there in the audience. Mine ain't with me here tonight, but his presence is always felt in my heart. *(Looks up at the starry ceiling)* This one's for you, Hoppy.

> *Sings Martina McBride's "Learning To Fall"*
> I was alone in the dark
> Never let down my guard
> Closed the curtain on my heart
> So the world could not see
> All the demons in me
> Told myself I was free
>
> Then you showed me how wrong I could be
>
> Now I'm standing on a mountain of rubble
> That once was a wall
> Took years to build around me
> And you came along
> And you tore it down
> Like it was nothing at all
> Now it's a little scary
> Learning to fall

When you looked in my eyes
Past the fear and false pride
You saw goodness inside
I can't believe how I feel
I believe love is real
And I'm ready to heal

You show me how right I can be

I was holding on, now I'm letting go
I was holding on, now I'm letting go
I was holding on, now I'm letting go

Everytime I close my eyes,
Sleeping ghosts of memories rise.
Painting portraits in my mind,
Of a love I've left behind.

Lights begin to fade on the Karaoke bar.
Spotlight holds on **YONG'S** *lifeless body for a couple of beats, then blackout.*
Disco ball is still on when the song is finished, holding for a few moments.
Blackout.
The "APPLAUSE" sign blinks on and off, then goes off once and for all.

SANG KIM

SANG KIM

SANG KIM